Beckenham

in old picture postcards volume 1

by
Muriel V. Searle

European Library – Zaltbommel/Netherlands

ISBN10: 90 288 4541 0
ISBN13: 978 90 288 4541 1

European Library
post office box 49
NL – 5300 AA Zaltbommel/The Netherlands
telephone: 0031 418 513144
fax: 0031 418 515515
e-mail:publisher@eurobib.nl

INTRODUCTION

Postcards were the telephone calls of yesterday; a universal medium for conveying short everyday messages. Most householders kept a stock always to hand for this purpose, showing the family's home town, or even their individual street; ideally, a card including their own house, marked with a cross by the sender in ink. Because these individual road views sold well, and therefore were extensively published, collectors can now build up a more comprehensive survey of any given town than would be possible through modern cards, limited to town centres. Post Office practice encouraged frequent use, with many collections and deliveries daily. It was possible to write a card in the morning and know it would be received within hours, especially on local services. For places like Beckenham and Shortlands one can thus build up a comprehensive record of their former appearance as country villages, and their later growth into suburbs. It is these two phases which are surveyed here; the third (their appearance since the Second World War) lies outside the scope of this series of books.

A suburb has been unkindly described as 'a town without a history', but this is far from true. Every square mile of land has some sort of past, based on the principal landowners, and the farmers who tenanted the fields before they were built over. The very trees sometimes speak of history, by originating placenames. Family names and village landmarks also helped create the modern Beckenham street map by perpetuating such terms as Village, Eden, Foxgrove, Kelsey, Gwydyr, Cator, Albemarle, Copers Cope, Elmers End, Manor or Rectory.

Beckenham's town name is variously attributed to its location: a ham or place by a beck or small stream; or else to one Beohha (Beohhahema), possibly pronounced as Becca – Becca's home or settlement. From a wild and lonely Saxon territory, where a handful of rough men lived by hunting and fishing, it progressed into a hamlet worthy of inclusion in Domesday Book, given by William the Conqueror to his half-brother, the odious Odo. By then it numbered a population of thirty and was worth £9 in rates.

Thereafter its growth was predictable for an English country village; centred on the manors of Foxgrove and Beckenham, and on a church that was rebuilt more handsomely in the fourteenth century and dedicated – like its modern successor – to our patron saint, St. George. The powerful Cator and Burrell families emerged, leaving their mark in further modern placenames. But not until the 19th century did it really begin to move towards township, after the coming of railways; suddenly, it was too near London to escape progress, and its picturesque main street and lush meadows were doomed.

At the 1871 census the population was already 6,090 and the parish covered 2,881 acres: a 'pleasant suburban village (that) has lost much of its old-fashioned rusticity and seclusion since the opening of the railways'. A report of 1873 put the town's rateable value at £72,373, and still rising; it added with accurate foresight: 'In all probability building would go on for many years in each of the four building centres.' The roads, in poor condition, urgently needed attention, not to mention sanitation, as local ditches were 'frequently used for the reception of sullage'.

The half-town, half-country state lasted until the second great building boom of the 1930s, again based on easy railway access: in this case, on recent electrification, bringing Beckenham even nearer, in journey time, to London. Its range of stations rivalled Croydon in number, including Beckenham Junction, New Beckenham, Beckenham Hill, Ravensbourne, Kent House, Clock House, Elmers End and Eden Park. The last countryside sank under a network of new genteel suburban villas, many in mock-Tudor style, selling for between £600 and £800, compared with a mere £400 down in 'poor class' Catford. Some cost £1,000; 'They'll never sell them at that price,' said the critics, but sell they did, and now fetch anything up to £250,000.

The former surrounding hamlets likewise grew and were linked up, notably at Shortlands, Elmers End and Langley, whose separate identities disappeared. This great explosion of house building joined them to each other, and also to Beckenham and Bromley, in one suburban sprawl. Of these, only Shortlands miraculously keeps something of its old character, where the main street is still called The Village. Though it straddles the former Beckenham/Bromley borders, with Queen's Mead and The Village on 'the wrong side of the railway', this is only a matter of yards inside the surviving Bromley boundary stones (one placed hard against the north side of Hillside Road footbridge, and another against a house in Bromley Gardens), and Shortlands as a whole keeps a subtle allegiance to Beckenham. It grew very much in the spirit of the latter emergent suburb, genteel and moneyed, and rich in huge Victorian mansions, quite different from the roads of artisan villas north of the railway.

Tradition even ascribes the pavements walked by Shortlands people to this old rivalry between two towns that are now one. Streets here and in Beckenham still tend to be pink paved, compared with commercialised Bromley's grey. Until modern local government changes, residents of such borderline areas as Valley Road and Queen Anne Avenue paid some official bills to Beckenham Town Hall and others to Bromley, keeping a foot in each camp.

All these facets of local life can be followed by collecting historic picture postcards, whose heyday lasted from the accession of Edward VII through to the Second World War. After the war, the new universality of telephones, previously limited mainly to commerce and the newly-rich, eliminated their purpose as carriers of simple daily messages, and therefore also the wide scope of scenes portrayed. Which seems good enough reason for turning back to that fascinating heyday period when rural Beckenham was changing faster than ever before, and its surrounding hamlets were caught up in its race towards modernity, destroying in a couple of decades almost everything of historic worth in favour of road after road of all-alike villas.

Only through surviving pictures can we now savour the sight of horses and carts in these streets, pedestrians in flowing skirts and tight corsets, and a pace of life that our generation has never known, and probably never will.

1. Modern residents sometimes find it difficult to visualise this place as a pretty little country town that might have been a hundred miles from London; yet this was its face within some old people's memories. This card shows not only the old wooden cottages (a fairly common postcard subject, but usually taken from the opposite angle), but also some of their mellow and gracious neighbours. The notion of commercialised shopping parades the whole length of the old High Street, with traffic and buses roaring past, would have seemed like a nightmare science fiction to the handful of villagers gathered here. However, there are certain signs of change. The road surface is comparatively smooth, and there are even pavements; yet a few decades earlier one Mr. Kick had needed to petition the local Works Committee for a pavement outside his shops; the work, costing all of £20, was agreed.

2. 'Beckenham is rapidly developing into a great and populous centre of modern suburban life and enterprise,' wrote a journalist of 1892. Though plenty of countryside remained between here and West Wickham, westward towards Penge and eastward towards Bromley its suburbanisation was by then well-advanced. Here the main street appears much as it looked up to the bombing of the 1940s, whose aftermath of replacement buildings began the modern breaking down of traditional Beckenham. Waiting at the left is a breed now virtually extinct outside the newspaper trade: the suburban errand boy with his cycle, which carries a sign advertising his employer's name and business. The little shops and background block at right are intact; apart from something of the left foreground shops, everything else on that side is gone.

3. Modernism has destroyed much of traditional Beckenham, but here it never had a chance: Hitler struck first, blitzing most of the right-hand side to nothing. The large bomb-site adjacent to St. George's – itself heavily damaged – long remained undeveloped, but has recently been grassed over and planted, under the old-world name of Beckenham Green. Part of the more distant block was replaced by modern concrete; a section of the new ground floor was until about 1984 called The Golden Arrow: a public house named after the immortal glamour-train which once whizzed, under steam, beneath the adjacent bridge. It boasted the biggest pub sign for miles around, the complete top part of a genuine old style semaphore signal.

4. The two top pictures show best how Beckenham has changed; the High Street scene is unrecognisable now. The old arched building was then a popular curio shop. Charmingly dressed figures outside a Cottage Hospital that still looks cottage-like again suggest a distant country town rather than one barely ten miles from central London. This was a very early Cottage Hospital, opened in 1872 with just four beds to serve a tiny community of six thousand people; it admitted just twenty-six patients in its first year. For a mere sixpence (2½p) a day all but the poorest could afford advice and treatment 'combined with a more liberal diet, ampler space, fresher air, and greater comforts than would be possible in their own homes'. By 1895 it boasted an operating room and seventeen beds. Even now, patients enjoy a pleasant outlook, as some wards overlook Croydon Road Recreation Ground (bottom right view).

5. A townscape filmed shortly after 1900, reasonably familiar still in its essentials: except for the total lack of traffic. A plaque here records the date of building the Public Hall, reading: 'This foundation Stone was laid by Sir C H Mills, Bart., MP, on the 13th October 1883.' At that period Local Government was expanding continuously to keep pace with the first of Beckenham's times of fast growth. Until 1872 the customary Vestry acted as a town council, after which civic affairs passed to a Rural Sanitary Authority, a Parochial Committee of 1874, and then to the more powerful Beckenham Local Board in 1878.

6. A leafy and more romantic interpretation of the Public Hall and Old Council Hall, made specially interesting by horse traffic. The unusually tall stone milepost on the corner was almost wrecked some years ago by a non-stop vehicle, hit so violently as to be cut off below ground level. Being such a prized piece of local history, in a town that has let so much of its past vanish, it was replaced on a slightly less vulnerable site, on the opposite corner. At the time of this picture much of the old Beckenham remained which is lost today, including the stately Village Place and picturesque Parish Clerk's House.

7. 'The Baths Question at Beckenham' occupied much local paper space when early in 1886 it was hotly debated: did Beckenham want or need a swimming bath? A 'meeting of ratepayers and owners of property' heard that £1,275 would be the price of this facility, including the cost of buying land, which could not be recovered for nineteen years; the estimated first year's loss of £246 would mean an extra halfpenny on the rates. One major consideration was that public baths had been tried on the Cottage Hospital site and failed; but not an actual swimming bath. The resolution that 'it is desirable to establish public baths in Beckenham under the Local Board' was on this occasion lost by 30 to 68 votes. This view shows the baths as finally adopted and built.

8. A horse-bus trundles along the road from central Beckenham towards Penge, the only vehicle in sight. Before a direct bus linked Bromley and Croydon, commuters between those towns were compelled to take a slow horse-bus like this down through Beckenham to Penge, and there change to another horse-drawn vehicle for the onward leg to Croydon. Both stages seemed weary treks, especially when the lower deck was full, and passengers were forced to sit on the open top deck, whatever the weather or season. Those days linger on still in the bus conductor's regular cry 'Outside only!' (as an alternative to 'On top only!') even though the upper seats are no longer outside and unroofed. During the General Strike of 1926, when motor buses stopped, young secretaries and shopgirls working in Croydon were expected, by hard employers, to walk all the way home to Beckenham, or even on to Bromley, until private transport could be arranged.

9. An impressive view posted in 1910, showing the stately splendour of the then Town Hall, later known as the Public Hall. The ornate roof is most unusual in England, strongly suggesting civic architecture in Flanders or Holland; as does the hall-like upper floor. At the turn of the century this and the adjoining building (at right) were used as a public hall and Local Board offices, whilst the next one in line, a fine corner block, was owned by the then London & County Bank; the latter is still a bank, the National Westminster. The long sheltered front verandah has disappeared, and also the ornamental rooftop cupola.

10. ‘When is the spire to take the place of that unsightly wooden cap?’ asked an important local gazetteer in the 1890s, six years after most of the present handsome Parish Church was completed. The lower stages of the tower can here be seen, up to the nave roof level, unsatisfactorily topped by this unworthy temporary version of a ‘Kentish Cap’. The right side of the road is still fairly familiar, but the old brick wall and few country type shops at left long ago vanished, replaced by today’s shopping parades. However, the flight of steps and raised embankment planted with shrubs are recognisable, keeping something of a less suburbanised Beckenham than we know today.

11. Church Hill; a card postmarked 1906, soon after completion of the new St. George's. The charming village church has been replaced by the majestic town church that is familiar today; urban shopping parades appear on the right and again at the left. The left-hand trees and wall, however, still look countrified compared to the modern shops that replaced them. The traffic – or lack of it – again suggests the last days of Beckenham as a country town, as does the only lightly made-up road surface. The now familiar police station, approached up attractively mellowed steps in the right background, was built in 1884.

12. This upward view looks towards St. George's Church from the lowest part of the High street; a part always liable to flooding. Boats have several times been rowed around this hollow, prone to trap water off this and the High Street gradients, and from a now hidden stream. A particularly vicious visitation occurred in 1878 when flood water lapped the tops of shop counters, and goods floated out of the doors and away down the street. Low-lying Shortlands has a similar history of flooding, culminating in the disaster of September 1968; in some houses then, water was level with table tops inside the rooms. As a result, widespread prevention measures were taken in the Ravensbourne Valley, all the way from Bromley, past Beckenham, and to the Thames confluence at Deptford; these included culverting, canalisation, and deepening.

13. Little now remains of pre-20th century Beckenham, but for the ancient George and the picturesque Kelsey Square. But within older living memory cottage shops like these still existed, alongside landed detached properties in spreading gardens, facing onto the old High Street. All were long since replaced by shops. They included the lovely Old Wood House, divided up into three shops, but believed to have originally been one single unit. The visual unity of a Kentish yeoman's hallhouse was born out on its demolition, when the internal structure was revealed; a single building with one fireplace and no chimney; a primitive gap in the roof allowed the smoke to rise. Old Wood House was situated about where W.H. Smith's shop is now. Other lost High Street gems included the Parish Clerk's House, demolished in about 1928 for 'improvements', and a fine Manor House.

14. Superficially a similar view, but with differences marking the march of development. Over the central alley a sign advertises the entry to Padbury's Carriage & Motor Works, confirming the changeover from horses; there was still some work done there with carriages and wagon wheels, and also horse-shoeing, but business must move with the times and cash in on the rise of motoring, by catering for both. A third grade of transport is in evidence, the bicycle. The business of A. Shepherd combined repair shops with dealership in the current popular makes, and also advertised over the window 'Cycles on Hire'. Behind the standing figures is a laundry office, more common in high class Beckenham than in working Penge. When laundering a sheet cost one penny (⅓p9, a lady of shop managerial status and above could send most of her household linen out and still receive a bill of little over 1s.6d (7½p) a week.

15. An interesting account survives of the St. Paul's Church dedication festival of 27th January 1880. 'The large number of carriages outside testified that the congregation consisted of a large number of the elite of the neighbourhood,' it was said, a reminder that St. Paul's lay in the smart part of Beckenham. Massed choirs from other local churches were joined by voices from the Chapel Royal, led by no less a musician than the Chapel Royal organist. The order of service was copied from a festival at the namesake St. Paul's Cathedral of 1878 with emphasis on the best in church music, including elaborate anthems and choruses; a string orchestra added to the lavish effect. On the other hand, the sermon by Canon Baynes broke Victorian convention by being 'short and eloquent'. So many gentry attended that the collection paid the heavy musical expenses, and also swelled the church's own choir funds.

16. This lovely church initially stood on an open country hilltop, serving those big properties in spreading grounds whose names live on in local street names, such as Hillside, Kingswood and Ravensbourne. It was consecrated in 1870, to serve this emerging landed parish, long before the quiet 1920s residential roads came to hem it in. In 1940 a landmine badly damaged it; four years later the remains were totally destroyed by a doodlebug, which was watched by residents of Hillside Road and Queen Anne Avenue as it barely cleared their homes, but it glided on in ominous silence, onto the church, exploding it into millions of fragments. The present replacement was consecrated in 1955 in the presence of the Mayor of Beckenham, Councillor Duncan, and the Lord Mayor of London, Alderman (later Sir) Cuthbert Ackroyd; the latter was much connected with this area, and resident at Widmore. He unveiled a commemorative plaque during the service.

17. St. Mary's, Shortlands, was designed in the revived English Gothic style; with a traditional lychgate, it gave the impression of being older than it really was. The church was totally destroyed in 1944, following severe damage by an earlier air raid. For some years it was possible for anyone reasonably active to climb to the top of the spire without special gear and down the other side; this was because it lay almost intact on the ground, where it had fallen. A new St. Mary's, in a very light modern hall style, occupies the same site, facing the original war memorial at a nearby road junction, where a very large scale outdoor Remembrance Service is held every November.

18. St. George's Beckenham in a halfway state in about 1902-03, during rebuilding of the pretty old village church. Church building has for centuries been started always at the east end, comprising the sanctuary and chancel; the setting of the high altar was completed first, followed by transepts and nave, and finally by a tower or spire. Here St. George's apsidal chancel is complete but as yet the noble tower now dominating central Beckenham is missing. Chief of Beckenham old church's features was Mary Wragg's Charity, distributed on 28th January. It involved payments to the Curate and parish officers in return for annually opening Mary Wragg's tomb, entering the family vault, inspecting it for needful repairs, and dusting the coffin. Any remaining cash after repairs was distributed, including 18d (7½p) worth of beef, 18d worth of bread, five shillings (25p) worth of coals, and 4.6d (22½p) in money, to twenty poor of the parish.

19. A nice close view of the strange wooden 'Kentish Cap' used to temporarily top off the new parish church tower when work came to a halt. Local opinion put this situation down to finance, but asked somewhat sarcastically whether so rich a parish as Beckenham, with more wealthy residents than any other for miles around, could really be hard up for this money. By the time of this picture, the tower seems to have been in this condition for about a decade; for the above question was asked in 1892, when tower building had already been at a halt for six years.

20. A small insignificant plaque overhead on a beam, as one enters this specially historic lychgate, briefly tells the story of this remarkable survival from the past: it is 'probably the oldest remaining in England', dating from about the 13th century. It was, of necessity, heavily repaired in 1924, but the magnificent main framework was not altered. As the inscription explains, 'the decayed ground cills and the bottoms of the side-posts were renewed on new foundations, and the spurs to the brackets, which had long been absent, were restored'. Today, old and new work are blended in unity, by age, wind and weather.

21. A picture dating from before the postcard age, but issued anew in postcard form as part of a series published by a well-known Beckenham printing and publishing company. It shows the ancient lychgate, but the notion of a towering town church here, or motor traffic where the cows wander with the perverse aimlessness of cattle, would have then seemed unimaginable as science fiction – had such a form of reading then existed. Even into the early 19th century cattle were still seen in Beckenham High Street, where the traditional pound was once used for rounding up stray cows until collected by their farmer owners.

22. Until the 1860s Beckenham was a single compact parish, centred on the one parish church of St. George, believed to date at least from Edward III's reign, and probably earlier still. When it was rebuilt, into the above form, the work was done in stages, always leaving part of the old building still accessible for use; it is held that, throughout those years of upheaval, not one service ever failed to be said or sung. First the chancel was rebuilt. In 1887 a second stage completed the nave and aisles. Not until 1902, as a fourth stage, was the uncompleted tower raised to full height, as seen here, and finished in 1903; the old bells were then recast and rehung.

23. By 1904, when this postcard was mailed, the corner of Church Hill looked much as it does today, with the tower at last completed. Beckenham's village image was almost banished, already well-removed from the days when the stocks (for errant inhabitants) and the pound (for rounding up cattle straying in the High Street) had been regularly used. A proper police station (now found at the right, just below this point) had taken over duty from the old cage, used to imprison and sober up the few local drunks. Beckenham's historic stocks were reproduced for an Olde Englishe Fayre in Coronation year (1953), when an old style village fair occupied much of the High Street, like a country fair of pre-traffic days.

24. Street names and public house names usually reflect a town's past, particularly prominent people and old estates and landmarks. Foxgrove Road, for instance, perpetuates the ancient manor of Foxgrove, documented at least as far back as the fourteenth century. Four centuries later it came into the Burrell family, again a prominent name on the modern street map. Before suburbanisation the only side road between St. George's Church and the Beckenham Place estate was that to Foxgrove Farm, lying approximately where The Avenue and Foxgrove Road were built. This romanticised view of Foxgrove Road, postmarked 1914, captures the select quietness of Edwardian Beckenham, with only one elegant pedestrian and horse-drawn vehicle in sight.

25. The origin of Coper's Cope as a placename has long puzzled local historians. Who was Coper, and why a cope, unless he was a priest? General opinion now favours a copse of trees and bushes, prominent when this was all farmland: Cope's, Coper's or Cooper's Copse. Coper's Cope Road perpetuates the elusive Mr. Coper or Cooper, and also the once extensive Coper's Cope Farm. This covered a huge 250 acres of countryside on the Kent and Surrey borders, right across the land now called New Beckenham, joining up by footpaths with Kent House Farm. After the building booms that turned a village into a London suburb, only Coper's Cope farmhouse remained, marooned uneasily amid new properties at the junction of Southend Road and Coper's Cope Road. This card shows the scene in 1910.

26. The one-time rolling countryside between Shortlands, West Wickham and Beckenham has been since the 1920s one continuous network of quiet high-class suburban roads, of which Malmains Way is a good example. Its name recalls how the Malmains family once owned the widespread Langley manor, from very soon after the Conquest. This family died out less than three centuries later, in 1350; but now, more than six centuries later still, their name is revived on the street map of modern Beckenham. Another road named after owners of Langley was Raymond Road, for Hugh Raymond, again of the old Langley estate and also of Elmer Lodge, which became the Manor House Club in Dunbar Avenue.

27. One of those well-heeled looking roads giving Victorian and Edwardian Beckenham the reputation for high class living. In the 1880s, when these properties were fairly new, a typical estate agent's advertisement would describe them as having up to eight bedrooms, separate dressing and bath rooms (when poorer class terrace cottages rarely owned more than a tin tub), three or more reception rooms, and 'ample offices, cellarage etc.' The setting would be described as grounds rather than a mere garden; one such house, 'Southview' in The Avenue, when auctioned in 1886 was said to also possess 'a tennis lawn, shrubbery, fernery and a productive kitchen garden; also a greenhouse and forcing-house'. Another good selling point was The Avenue's proximity to Beckenham Junction, with trains to the City starting at 5.09 am and giving about twenty-five services daily in each direction.

28. The Avenue in the 1920s, still very much a 'good address', though by then the fashionable mock-Tudor element was creeping in among the stately older properties, as seen in the house at the right. A fine new property like this might sell for about £800, or even £1,000; an astronomical figure compared with the small £400 villa in, say, Catford. By then it was becoming more common for ordinary clerk-class husbands to take a mortgage on the smaller and cheaper house, whereas before the Great War the majority of less moneyed families only paid rent, continually moving house as their leases ran out. Earlier still, even the better properties were commonly rented rather than bought; a larger house in The Avenue or Copers Cope Road was priced at about £125 a year in rent just before the turn of the century.

29. Kings Hall Road, a good example of the middle bracket of early town housing, neither mansions nor cottages, but good solid family homes. Owners like these were not rich, but could nevertheless afford certain assets outside the reach of the shopkeeper and artisan classes, like a maid-of-all-work (sometimes spoken of simply as The Woman, without even a surname, by a patronising mistress); or perhaps a governess to teach such added refinements as music, poetry, painting, needlework, embroidery or dancing. Local papers between about 1870 and 1930 were always full of advertisements for such tutors, giving addresses in the better roads of Beckenham. These non-academic subjects were known as accomplishments and taught mainly to young ladies in the making.

30. This long road running in the direction of West Wickham – as its name implies – looks strangely unfamiliar in its emptiness. It typifies the common conception of residential Beckenham as a well-bred, moneyed district of comfortably placed business and professional men, needing large houses with room for servants as well as family. Like similar roads in Sydenham and Norwood, this area became desirable after the rebuilding of the Crystal Palace on Sydenham Hill, attracting the better classes by its initital dedication as a centre of the arts and sciences.

31. Beckenham looked like this a mere sixty years or so ago: a placid Kentish village surrounded by rich meadows with limpid streams, and rolling hills. Though romanticised, this picture speaks much truth. The background range may represent the great wooded ridges of Sydenham, away from the Crystal Palace, seen from the pastoral meadows of either Elmers End or what is now New Beckenham. This idyllic scene recalls a description of 1892: 'The air is pure and fresh, and free from the smoke and dust with which that of London is surcharged.' The village was equally rural: 'A cleanly appearance, and the abundance of foliage, verdant lawns, and gardens glowing with bright colours give the whole scene a very fresh, lively and inviting tone.'

32. This peaceful country house is simply described as being in Bromley Road, Beckenham, probably near the turn of the 19th and 20th centuries. The idyllic scene gives no hint of the suburbia to come, swallowing innumerable pretty villages whose only mistake was to be set too near London. As late as 1875 it could be said: 'The neighbourhood is... still agreeable: it abounds in trees, the surface is undulating, and there are tempting field and lane walks to Bromley, Hayes and Wickham.' Indeed, when one side of Queen Anne Avenue at Shortlands was built in 1930, the opposite side was still so open that newly-wed residents could leave their garden gates and walk through open country to West Wickham; a situation that lasted only two or three more years. Thereafter, Shortlands suburbia linked to Bromley suburbia and that of Beckenham: a process repeated at Elmers End, Langley, New Beckenham, Eden Park; indeed, wherever there was even one more meadow available.

33. Clock House today is just a station name and a nondescript district between Beckenham and Penge; but this was the placid place responsible for these names on the modern map. The namesake clock crowned a range of stables near the site of an older house, and was owned by one of the ubiquitous Cators; a magnificent mature magnolia climbed up one wall, increasing the air of an English country mansion. The house did not survive the turn of the 19th and 20th centuries. Two fragments of Clock House did remain; a fine double tiered fountain from the lake, placed in a smaller pond in Croydon Road Recreation Ground; and the pretty little clock tower itself, taken from the stables by the Cator family in 1896 and added to a similar range of buildings at Beckenham Place (now a golf course), placed to crown the roof of the mellow old block facing the formal gardens.

34. This card is captioned vaguely 'Near Bromley, Kent', but the general character suggests the unsuburbanised River Ravensbourne on the Beckenham side of that town – probably somewhere between Shortlands and Southend; the river would have been much narrower above Bromley. Up to the mid-1920s local people could walk or cycle from either town, all the way to Catford through this exquisite pastoral valley, seeing only fields but for the occasional inn and the tiny hamlet of Southend (at the extreme south end of Catford). All this loveliness was transformed into suburbia in the later 1920s and early 1930s; the river, of course, still flows, but culverted under some roads, canalised behind back gardens or, even when it crosses sports grounds, dug down and more formalised. The Ravensbourne in this dream of a picture has gone for ever.

35. From the top of Beckenham Church tower one would hardly expect to see open fields today, nor the fabulous Crystal Palace. Before modern flying, the high lying Palace grounds were much used by balloonists, ascending before vast crowds of onlookers, drifting silently off over Beckenham. Most of Beckenham's small population rushed outside when on 21st August 1886 four men in a basket dangling under a majestic balloon, flying from Woolwich to the Palace, scarcely cleared the cottage roofs, so low that greetings could be shouted to them. Finally the balloon flopped to earth in a brickfield at Kent House, after helplessly circling Bromley in unfriendly wind currents. Mr. Bocock, manager of the Crystal Palace gasworks, hurried to Kent House to safely drain off the gas before carting the balloon away. Beckenham village rarely saw excitement as this.

36. Each London suburb initially developed out of a separate village, eventually all linked into a single sprawl, but only during the past century. Even inner areas like Camberwell or Clapham emerged this way; Beckenham, farther out, took longer to lose its country origins; not during the first main suburb-building boom, but in the second, from about 1925 to 1935. Here is a delicious remaining footpath, as it still looked in about 1909. 'Until comparatively recent times there was scarcely even a village in Beckenham,' it was said not long before this picture was taken. Here the wide Langley estate sets the geography of a long-lost scene; covering a vast 3,202 acres, it ran from Ham Farm (namesake of this foothpath) and Monks Orchard on one side to Beckenham centre and even onwards towards Bromley.

The Abbey, Beckenham. Dining Hall.

37. Beckenham, like Bickley, developed the 'posh' character of the Victorian/Edwardian suburb of money and fashion. It had many huge houses employing several servants, and running one or more carriages. Such families wanted the best of snob-appeal schools for their children, especially sons, and various expensive private establishments soon appeared. Chief of these was The Abbey, described in 1892 as the biggest and best private school in Kent. Placed near Beckenham Junction, it was founded in 1866 by the Reverend Lloyd Phillips. Boys had private dormitory cubicles, and even a carpentry shop. There was a separate sanatorium with isolation unit, for even in the best areas typhoid, diphtheria and cholera were not yet stamped out. The lavishly appointed dining room seen here resembles an Oxford college hall, housing many pictures and also the school's array of sporting trophies.

38. A gentleman's son's schooling included developing a cultured accent, a sense of superiority, and learning to 'Play The Game'. The Abbey School encouraged the latter with outstanding sports facilities. It boasted nine acres of grounds, plus a cricket club and private swimming pool. Compared with Elementary and Board Schools attended by ordinary children, who might be turned away if unable to produce their weekly penny (⅓p) fee, and where learning was based mainly on the Three R's, The Abbey came nearer to a public school. Indeed, many boys went on to Eton, Harrow, Winchester or Rugby; or to Oxford, or into naval officer courses.

39. Balgowan in about 1916. This and several other names on the map derived from the Boer War, which was taking place at about the time that these roads were built. The name Balgowan came from the town of Balgowan, near Pietermaritzburg. The adjoining Belmont Road was named after Belmont, south of Kimberley, notable for a major battle fought in 1899. Durban Road again recalled the Boer War, this being the main entry port for British troops ferried across from the India of the Raj. Colesburg Road took its title from Colesberg (spelled with an 'e' instead of 'u'), situated in Cape Province.

40. Queen's Mead lies 'on the wrong side of the railway', technically within Bromley by a whisker; but it is still locally regarded as definitely Shortlands, while the background hill is definitely part of Bromley. All these noble trees died of Dutch elm disease in the 1970s. The pretty River Ravensbourne was harshly canalised after the savage 1968 flood cost many of us part of our homes; the rustic bridge, by then replaced by spiked railings, was again replaced, this time by concrete. Near here long trestle tables were laid out for a huge outdoor party of Shortlands children to celebrate Edward VII's coronation. Old residents recall the strangely unchildlike rhyme they learned to sing: *We'll all be merry/ Drinking whisky, wine and sherry/ On Coronation day/ On Coronation Day.*

41. Though this view of about 1915 is captioned Bromley, and taken from there, nearly all the scenery below lies in Shortlands (middle fields), Clay Hill (centre trees) or Beckenham (distance), with the Crystal Palace on the skyline. Even though much building happened in the 1920s and 1930s, and a minor spate of flat building more recently, the general appearance of the view today is not far removed from that meeting the eye of the man in a straw hat. H.G. Wells as a boy sat up here, looking over the stream he only loosely disguised as the Ravensbrook in 'The New Machiavelli', running towards Beckington (Beckenham).

42. Beckenham's main stately home, seen here in about 1915, has long been a golf club house; the vast grounds are preserved both for golf, and also as natural fields, hills and bluebell woods. The statues flanking the door vanished since the war. This seat of the wealthy Cators was the setting of a formal 18th century social life, attracting people of both brains and beauty. They included Dr. Johnson; the great Swedish botanist Linnaeus, who added exotic plants and shrubs to the gardens; and Fanny Burney of 'Evelina' fame, who described Cator as a chatterer. The wit Mrs. Thrale drew up a cynical 'school report' on John Cator, based on twenty points; he earned nil for religion, morality, scholarship, manner, wit and humour, but thirteen points for general knowledge. He died in 1806 with no male heir; the estate went to a nephew, John Barwell Cator of Clock House.

43. These twin lodges (matched by a similar pair opposite Beckenham Hill station) now lead to Beckenham Place as a golf club house, instead of a private mansion; but they are still recognisable, if no longer so creeper covered as in this scene postmarked 1903. Continuing by this drive – now flanked beyond the lodges by very lavish and expensive private detached houses – one enters the golf course. Near the brow of the drive survives the Place's mysterious pond, heavily fenced as a danger. Legend calls it bottomless, though fact suggests a remarkable thirty feet, despite its small circumference; curiously, no life is observed except for one corner, populated by newts and tadpoles. The surrounding mud is described as like quicksand, capable of sucking a child or dog under within minutes; hence the fencing.

44. Kelsey, whose grounds now form Kelsey Park, was the town's most extravagant and exciting mansion: turreted and ivy-clad, a cross between a Scottish baronial pile and a romantic Loire château. Though the mansion was reworked in this final form during the 19th century period of Gothic romance, the actual estate dated from the early 15th century, if not earlier. Outlying parts of this great estate included Kelsey Park Farm, near the Cottage Hospital, which was bought in 1946 for staff accommodation; the last of the Hoare financier family to live at Kelsey was a founder member of the hospital trustees, a committee set up in 1871. Kelsey became one of Beckenham's military hospitals during the Great War, after which the noble mansion deteriorated, and was eventually demolished.

45. 'Rather a pretty spot' wrote the sender of this card in 1909: and it is still pretty. But who, seeing this usually placid lake and its lower companion, would suspect either of savagery? During the unforgettable 1968 flood both overflowed muddily across the landscape and surged into the town, recalling those 19th century floods when boats were often rowed at that lowlying point. Old byelaws for Beckenham's parks now make amusing reading; among other things, they forbade women from washing clothes in the lakes, or polluting the public drinking fountains; others forbade public grazing of sheep, cattle or pigs, and the admission of verminous and unwashed vagrants.

46. Most of Kelsey Park's paths were for decades enclosed by this rustic fencing, much of it now removed to give a less formal feeling. Here the photographer is looking from above the main waterfall. At dusk on a winter afternoon Kelsey can become almost spooky; the mournful clang of the patrolling keeper's bell was even eerier, rising and receding as he walked around calling out 'closing time'. His bell was a fragment of local history, taken from the old fire station when it stood at picturesque Kelsey Square, formerly the great mansion's main approach. This fire warning bell hung in a little turret above the station, and was removed when a larger new station (itself now obsolete and abandoned) was built. The ornate Kelsey Square since has played many roles; for years the lower part has been a country-style open fronted greengrocery shop; low down at its side is a bit of old Beckenham, an historic public pump.

47. Kelsey Park has two fine waterfalls; this lower fall, and the upper one of a single deep drop; from the point here pictured the two lakes drain into a river, prettily landscaped as it leaves the park. A description of the Ravensbourne penned in 1841 applied equally to the other brooks and streams of the Beckenham area, before the 20th century brought in housing to cancel out their surrounding meadows: 'Its banks are fringed by alders and willows, through which one can with but difficulty make way, and where the occasional whirr of the partridge as it starts suddenly from the ground... or of the pheasant mounting heavily upwards, speaks of the solitude that generally reigns...'

48. Strolling through the park on a card postmarked 1923. Croydon Road Recreation Ground was opened to the public in 1891; a benefit not only to the average mobile citizen, but equally to those confined in the adjacent Cottage Hospital, as it afforded 'a pleasurable and cheerful prospect from the wards', which by then could cope with nearly a hundred admissions a year. Between the two world wars this was the scene of some magnificent flower shows held in giant marquees, and attended by thousands of spectators. The floral displays were backed up by such additional attractions as band concerts, children's dancing displays on an open air stage, and a model steam hauled railway.

49. The heavy park architecture fashionable in the late 19th century is here shown in about 1905. Rustic public shelters, like the one at extreme left, were very characteristic of Beckenham's parks right through to about the 1960s, built solidly of timber, with long comfortable benches inside, divided into separate seats by wooden armrests, and usually prettily thatched. Sadly, the present trend towards vandalism made them the target of destroyers and arsonists, notably those shelters in nearby Kelsey Park; generally it has been necessary to replace them with more mundane brick or concrete structures.

50. A good example of the work of the Metropolitan Drinking Fountain & Cattle Trough Association's legacy of park installations. They date from a period before reliable public supplies, when running water was so contaminated by cholera and typhoid bacteria, especially in cities, as to be dangerous; one reason for reliance on cheap gin and beer. This campaign to bring clean wholesome water to public streets and parks put such fountains into almost every town park during Queen Victoria's reign. The horse troughs were strategically placed where weary working horses most needed a drink; locally they included one at Swan Hill, otherwise known as Beckenham Lane, and several on the long hills leading up to Crystal Palace.

51. Comic cards have always been uncommon for places other than seaside resorts: a suburban funny card is even rarer. Here the drunkard feeling his way home along some railings punningly suggests the area's wealth of rail connections. But even more interesting are all those that might have been, had their proposed enabling bills ever got through Parliament. Among these abortive schemes were the Beckenham Lewes and Brighton Railway; a line from Shortlands Junction to Eastbourne, abandoned as too costly because of hilly terrain; the Bromley Farnborough and West Wickham Railway; another from Lewisham to Croydon and Bromley, traversing parts of outer Beckenham; and a Farnborough (Kent) branch off the West End Of London & Crystal Palace Railway, one of the earliest companies to build through Beckenham towards Bromley.

52. This is Beckenham Junction before Southern Electrification by third rail during the 1920s. As far back as about 1870, local timetables included services denied to modern commuters for decades, unless recent prospects of a re-opening of the Snow Hill link materialise. London Chatham & Dover timetables show that an early train leaving Beckenham at 7.11 am (including stops at the now long-lost stations of Camberwell New Road and Walworth Road) reached Farringdon at 8.04; a weary limp of nearly an hour for about eleven miles; but then it took to a gallop, burrowing under London to reach Kings Cross (Midland) in only four minutes. Some trains also served the Kings Cross Great Northern section, opening the Midlands and North by means of an easy change. Running in the other direction, it could take four hours to crawl to Dover under steam, and over 3½ hours from Beckenham to Margate.

53. Kent House station, like Clock House, has lost the landmark house that originally decided its name; in this case, the first house in Kent when approaching from the west. Described in about 1874 as 'a fine old brick mansion', Kent House was then so rural that the shortest cut from it to Sydenham was by open field paths: an unimaginable situation today. Once Kent House Farm, after which was named Kent House Road, became a hotel; its site had been used for country houses since the 13th century. The slogan 'Southern Electric' dates this view to a time after amalgamation in 1923, creating the Southern Railway, and before its merger into BR in 1948. Electrification was a prime reason for the massive building boom which turned miles of countryside into miles of suburban roads; it brought London nearer than ever before, in terms of time, thus creating the commuter belt.

54. Costumes of the very early 20th century photographed in about 1901-1902 at Kent House, then a new suburb whose ranks of uniform small Victorian villas still form the greater part of the housing near Kent House station. As the name implies, the original house and the modern district named after it marked the site of the ancient boundary between Kent and Surrey, somewhere between Beckenham and Penge. In Lambarde's day it was identified by a stile. Other local names on this theme included Surrey Field, at the edge of Monk's Orchard estate (but a name probably older than that). This lay on the county boundary, but Monk's Orchard itself did not have the seemingly logical derivation. It did not come from any monastery, but from the Monk family of Addington, from over the Surrey border, who also were large landowners at West Wickham and Beckenham in Kent.

Ruby Verrell.

55. Ruby Verrell's Dainty Blossoms were a large and very well-known children's dancing troupe, performing throughout Beckenham, Bromley and district, especially between the two world wars, and on into about the 1950s. Their massed displays, spectacular for sheer numbers, were given mainly in church and public halls. Picture postcards of stage and (later) film stars circulated in thousands before TV made their features readily familiar to their public. Even more localised entertainers followed this trend, which publicised their talents and names, such as in this attractive Ruby Verrell card.

56. A Shortlands butcher's trade picture, probably taken early in the 20th century for publicity purposes. As recently as the 1950s Shortlands kept its true village shops, whereas today these are interspersed by addresses of convenience. They included a fishmongery whose floor was deep in clean sawdust, where a lady cashier sat imprisoned in state within an enclosed wood and glass cubicle. Another shop, a grocery, ran a simplified version of the once common overhead cash railway, whereby a cylinder containing the customer's bill and cash was catapulted along a wire into the cash desk and returned with the receipt and change; in larger stores quite complex networks evolved, with cylinders continually rocketing across at ceiling height by complete networks of wires.

57. Butchers in particular preserved the tradition of the annual trade photograph, taken when the shop was most fully stocked; it was usually reproduced in postcard form for local advertising and correspondence purposes. In this sample of a smaller shop, the staff of Sangster's in Shortlands Village pose with the usual ranks of flesh and fowl. They include an errand boy with his bicycle, at left, and a young butcher's boy at right, wearing a miniature trade apron; such boys were hired at very low pay of perhaps a shilling (5p) to 1s.6d. (7½p) a week to learn the trade and make themselves useful at odd jobbs.

58. Many cards were issued of Park Langley as a developing suburb, when smart new roads cut into the old estate, whose owners could be traced right back to the 1450s. It had survived partially intact up to 1904, when the remaining lands were split up and sold, though much of it was kept green in the form of Park Langley golf course. Players enjoyed the stateliest of club-houses, the magnificent ancient mansion, until it was tragically destroyed by fire in 1913. Today Park Langley is best known for its unique so-called Chinese Garage, which is actually in Japanese style; its charming pagoda roof and forecourt edged with oriental lanterns have recently been complemented in a modern road roundabout nearby, whose bollards have been designed to be in keeping, again in this unusual style.

59. A characteristic example of a medium sized older Beckenham property in its heyday. 'Fairlight' (Number 36 The Avenue, whose site is now taken for flats) housed the Link and Crosdale families, keen horticulturalists who could afford to employ two gardeners whose responsibilities included two or three greenhouses, growing such exotic plants as orchids; the master of the house expected a perfect orchid to be available each morning as a buttonhole. The mistress meanwhile indulged her passion for keeping canaries. Any house possessing spare rooms during the Great War was required to billet troops; such large ones as those in Albemarle Road might take in several; their pleasure was to shout across the intervening railway to children in the gardens of 'Fairlight', whose owner even invited them to use his immaculate croquet lawn. What greater contrast could there be than croquet and the coming carnage of Flanders?

60. 'During the past month a commencement has been made by instruction of Peter Hoare Esq., to erect a Cottage Hospital, to which it is intended to attach baths and wash-houses. This boon to the inhabitants of Beckenham cannot fail to be much appreciated. When will the like advantages be obtainable at Bromley?' asked the 'Bromley Record' in April 1869. In fact, Beckenham was among the first towns to adopt this idea. 'The institution has proved of great utility to the district,' it could be said only twenty years later. Even now it keeps a bit of its old appearance as seen from the road, though much enlarged behind this attractive frontage. The main patient entrance is still by the portico seen at right in this card dated 1918. Ward names often reflect local history; here they include a Stilwell Ward, a reminder that Doctor R. Stilwell was at one time Beckenham's only doctor. A descendant practiced in Manor Road until about 1980.

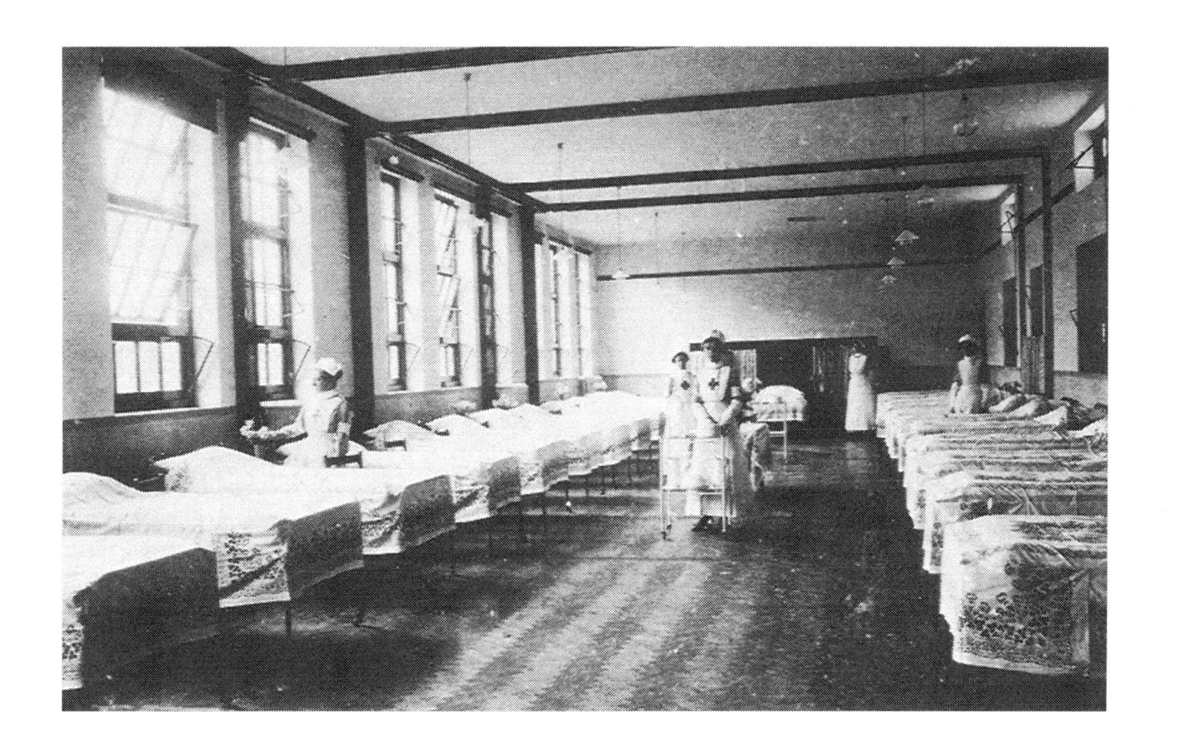

61. Balgowan School, a mixed primary school, was built in 1915: just in time to serve a totally contrasted purpose, as a military hospital, run by the Red Cross. This card appears to show a ward newly set up and awaiting the first wave of patients, with the beds made up but empty. Despite wartime restrictions and shortages, there are concessions to morale and comfort; each bed has an attractive floral cover.

62. A marvellously nostalgic scene from the First World War, showing a Beckenham ambulance crew in about 1916. Dr. Randall is on the far side, and Dr. George Stilwell in the foreground. Beckenham had at least three military hospitals during the war, at Balgowan School, Christ Church halls, and Kelsey mansion. The Cottage Hospital was directly interlinked with the Naval Brigade depot at the Crystal Palace, whose gigantic aisles were given over to billeting thousands of troops and naval men throughout the conflict. Its temporary name was H.M.S. Crystal Palace; as it was thus technically a ship, men going on leave or into military hospitals were described as going ashore.

63. Dr. Tim Randall in uniform during the Great War, whilst working at the Balgowan military hospital. Some medical families served Beckenham for two or three generations, including the Randalls and the Stilwells. Dr. R.M.H. Randall was an early board member and Honorary Medical Officer of the Cottage Hospital, from 1895 through to 1925; a span of three decades. Dr. Robert Stilwell, Beckenham's earliest GP, also worked for the Cottage Hospital, another early Medical Officer, from 1872 to 1887. His successors included Dr. George Stilwell, again involved in casualty medicine during the First World War.

64. Kingswood Road with very little housing, deserted but for a squad of troops apparently forming-fours in the middle of the road. During the Great War hundreds of men were officially billeted in Shortlands, Beckenham and Bromley; householders with even one unneeded room were required to take them in, and were paid an allowance for their keep. The Soldiers' Club at Bromley was centred on the Central Hall and Congregational Church; it was legendary for its hospitality and entertainment, attended by the billeted men from all over these three districts. Local musicians and entertainers gave their services and all manner of 'comforts' were given out. Concerts for troops were given at many local halls, such as the Public Hall at Beckenham or the various church halls there. The few mansion-like properties of old Kingswood Road are now complemented by the more expensive variety of 1930s housing.

65. The Old Cottage (formerly The Old Farmhouse), opposite Shortlands station, serenely stands aloof from the changes of the centuries: the development of tracks into highways, the coming of trains and buses, and two world wars. It still looks much the same, though all around it continually changes. Behind the trees (centre) was a great Edwardian house with elaborate conservatories, where one owner of the 1960s bred superb Afghan hounds. Legend associates the Cottage with the poet Shelley, believed to have changed horses there on visits to the prominent economist Ricardo, related to the owners of nearby Shortlands House (now Bishop Challoner School), to which a farm track ascended from this house. Along the main foreground road from Beckenham traffic now almost eternally runs, joined by more from the other road, controlled by lights placed where the single figure is pictured walking in about 1915.

66. Could ever Ravensbourne Avenue have looked like this? It did, in the early 1920s, and in fact the rough gravelly surface remained unmade until well after the Second World War, all the way to Ravensbourne; a country station more rural than many in the real country, even today, despite a recent fire. There begins the Beckenham Place estate, approached by a long drive from Ravensbourne. Ravensbourne Avenue has long been noted for its magnificent mature chestnut trees; less well-known now is the fact that a piggery existed in suburbia until some twenty years ago, directly under the high railway embankment approaching Shortlands, until replaced by two or three new houses wedged between the road and railway. Much open country survives behind the houses, where Shortlands golf course runs from The Village almost to Ravensbourne, joining with other sports fields and then with Beckenham Place Park.

67. Modern Shortlands developed, on both sides of the railway, primarily out of a handful of houses erected in 1865 in then lonely Kingswood Road, formerly part of the Shortlands Estate. It was first mentioned by name on a map of 1723. Until comparatively modern times, Shortlands House (now Bishop Challoner School) and The Old Cottage, still standing opposite the station, were the only buildings there. Ravensbourne Avenue links Shortlands and Ravensbourne stations, ending within sight of Beckenham Place Park. The lodge-like building at the right is still there.

68. An attractive old style street lamp – of which a few still exist in Shortlands – is a reminder that public lighting has only been common during the past century or less. Beckenham Local Board, meeting in January 1886, spent much time discussing 'the lighting of Shortlands'; a subject which had several times been debated and then shelved without action. Now it was revived, with the Surveyor recommending three extra lights in the village. And about time: Shortlands lagged behind eighteen other local parishes, paying a Lighting Rate but still without light. Only a couple of miles away 'Beckenham proper' was gaslit by about 1892, by two companies (from Bromley and Crystal Palace); and rumour believed that 'the fair young goddess Electra' was about to benefit the town. Electric light in fact reached Beckenham in 1900.

69. Today heavy traffic hurtles down this long hill towards Shortlands station. On the left are now several blocks of flats on a narrow triangular site between this road and the railway bank. Until about the 1960s their site was a horticultural nursery, whose long holly hedge survives. This locality is associated with Mrs. Craik, writer of 'John Halifax, Gentleman', whose adoption of a foundling was widely reported in 1869; the year that she and George Craik built The Corner House at Shortlands. Briefly, the young baby girl was heard crying by a gardener on his way to work on New Year's day, and found abandoned beside a heap of builders' bricks near Gloucester Terrace in School Road (St. George's Road). News spread, until 'two benevolent ladies, Miss Wilkinson of Shortlands and Mrs. Craik of Chilchester Lodge', elected to adopt it from the workhouse. She was baptised Dorothy, and finally taken by the authoress Mrs. Craik.

70. Even now Shortlands is leafy and pretty. The networks of residential roads between it and central Beckenham are quiet and pleasant, haunted by birds and squirrels, and shaded by massive old trees like these, left standing when houses took the place of hedgerows. Scotts Lane is here almost totally rural; today it is built up and well-groomed rather than natural.

71. A more suburbanised version of Scotts Lane, near the brow of the hill between Shortlands and Beckenham-proper, built up with rather expensive properties, and with the addition of appropriate street-furniture including a pillar-box. It is typical of the moderately well-to-do middle category of early 20th century development in Shortlands, between the top class mansions around St. Mary's and the smaller artisan cottages and houses placed in conventional rows on the other side of the railway, such as those of Recreation Road or Meadow Road.

72. The changeover of Shortlands from hamlet to residential village was duly chronicled by the local press. By 1869 it was assumed that its immediate future would be mainly that of a gentleman's retreat; which brought unexpected problems. Outward show came first, and such men could be surprisingly reluctant to invest money outside their own gates. Their fine carriages brought prestige, but also damage to the poorly made roads, as more and more hoofs and wheels ploughed them up. 'In this fashionable locality large houses are constantly springing up, and as a consequence the roads get worn and out of repair, and their present state is being much complained of,' said one journal. The gentry should honour their commitments: 'The owners of the several properties are bound by their terms of purchase to repair (the roads), and it is clearly to their comfort as well as interest in every sense to do so.'

73. 'A portion of the Shortlands Estate, 1½ miles east from old Beckenham Church, has... been built over, and a railway station and railway hotel opened,' it was recorded in 1875. By a railway hotel we presume the writer to have meant the Shortlands Tavern, almost directly alongside the present platform 4; its sign shows the first of Shortlands' two water works in Valley Road, with its now missing tall chimney; part of one of the works' heavy old beam engines is now preserved inside the fence in Valley Road. Shortlands Road – shown here – leads up from where Valley Road meets the station area, to join Hayes Lane where it enters Park Langley. The station forecourt, now only a car park, was occupied until just after the Second World War by the stationmaster's house; an attractive building whose gardens were noted for mature fig trees.

74. 'On the high ground by the church several good villas have been built,' was the updating phrase in a suburban gazetteer of about 1874, when Shortlands was in its infancy. But by the end of the century a pattern of residential roads was established. The Chalets, on the hilltop opposite St. Mary's, survive as a mellow brick fantasy, still with the deep upper balconies shown here, at right. On the opposite corner, out of the picture, another giant house was owned by the electrical pioneer Alexander Muirhead; today it bears a blue plaque commemorating his residence there. After 1918, the Shortlands war memorial was placed in the centre of this crossroads.

75. A famous murder of 1877 gave Forbes Road (renamed as Mosslea Road in an attempt to lessen the stigma) a wide notoriety, as the scene of the so-called Penge Murder; until the residents of one side of the road found that, by a few yards, it did not happen in Penge at all. The other side, including the murder house, officially lay in Beckenham. On this basis of an obscured boundary we feel justified in including two glimpses of old Penge. Here the High Street, seen in 1934, climbs towards the Palace gates. It looks impossibly far removed from the place in Domesday Book, a 'wood for fifty hogs pannage' (hence the name, Penge); or from an idyllic hamlet where the Croydon Canal crossed Penge Common, shaded by peaceful willows.

76. St. John's boys' school, Penge, seen in about 1909 with a tram leaving the picture and a horse bus entering it. The Surrey/Kent border and the Penge/Beckenham border lay in this vicinity. Just before the advent of railways Penge housed only 228 villagers; by the time of the Jubilees almost every acre was jam-packed with standardised working-class terraces, changing to roads of majestic semi-mansions near the Crystal Palace, and into high class avenues where servants and carriages were kept, on the opposite side where Penge merged into Kent House and Beckenham-proper. The few present reminders of its village days include an ornamental waterway in Betts Park, which is the sole surviving stretch of the old Croydon Canal; its banks were rural Penge's pleasantest pleasaunce, and the tea-gardens there were favoured by Londoners for a day of relaxation, deep in the heart of the country.